雷

Written and Illustrated By

Robert Louie

I AM MEMPŌ

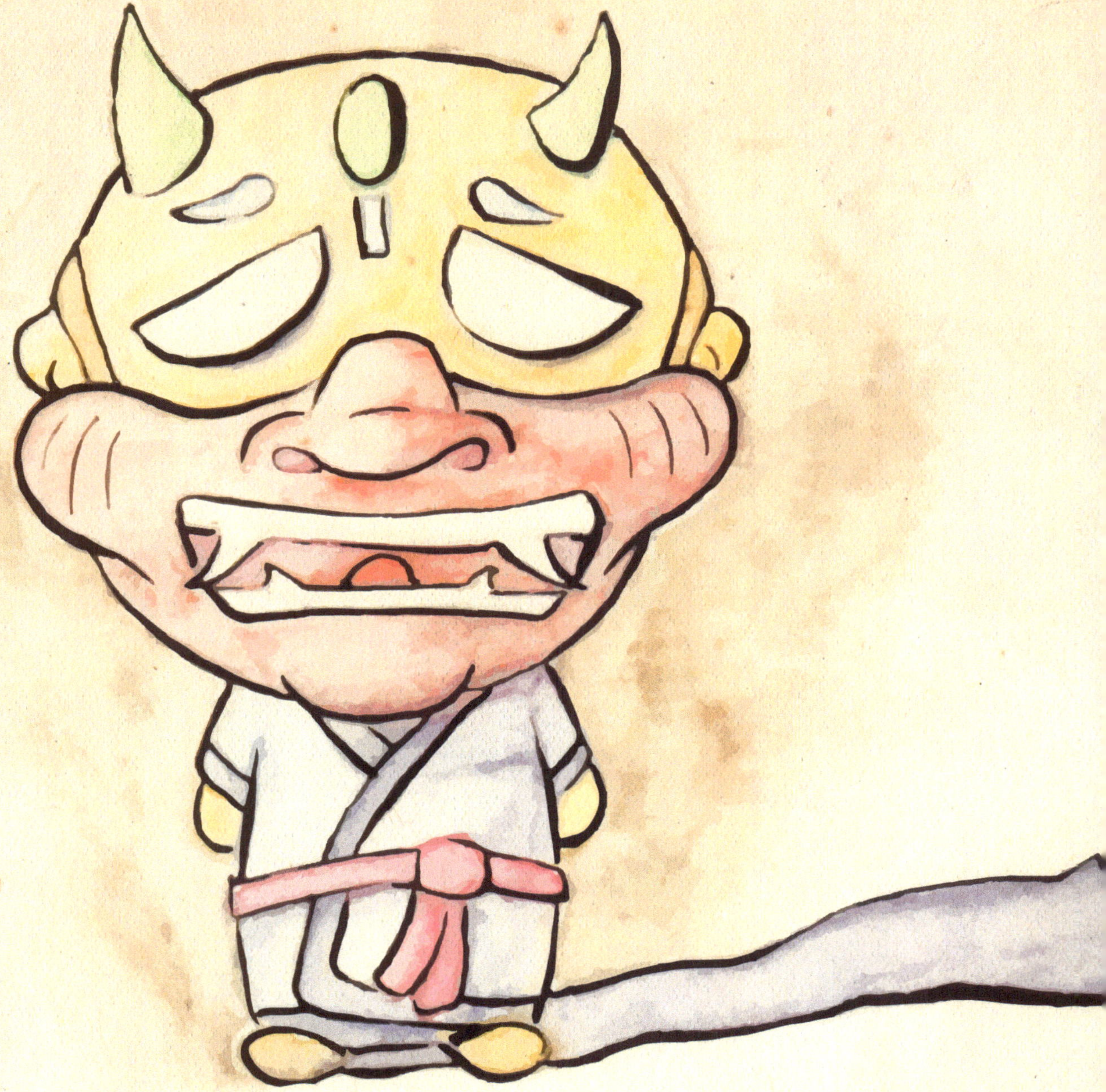

We Are ARMOR

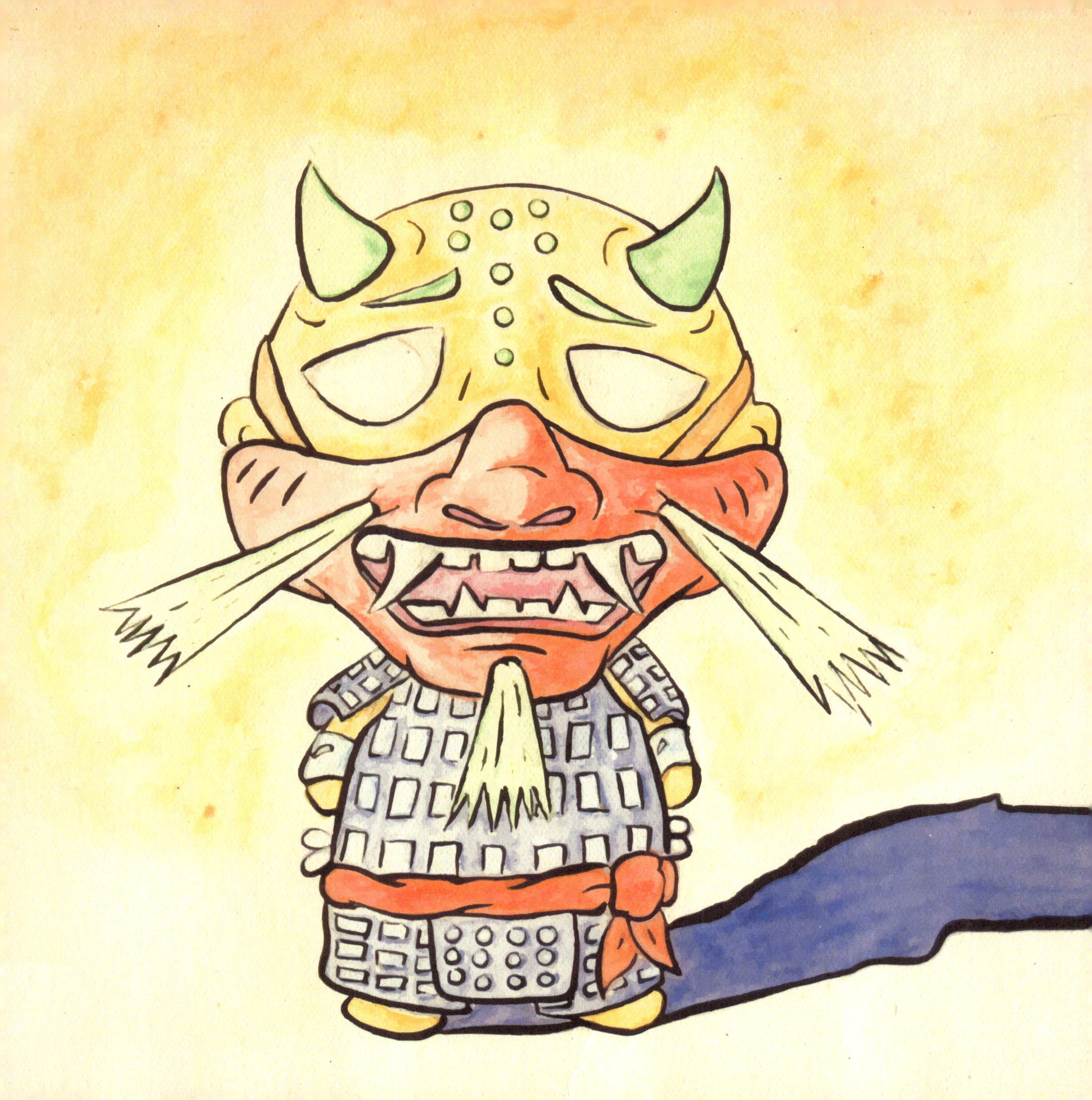

They Are Not Prepared

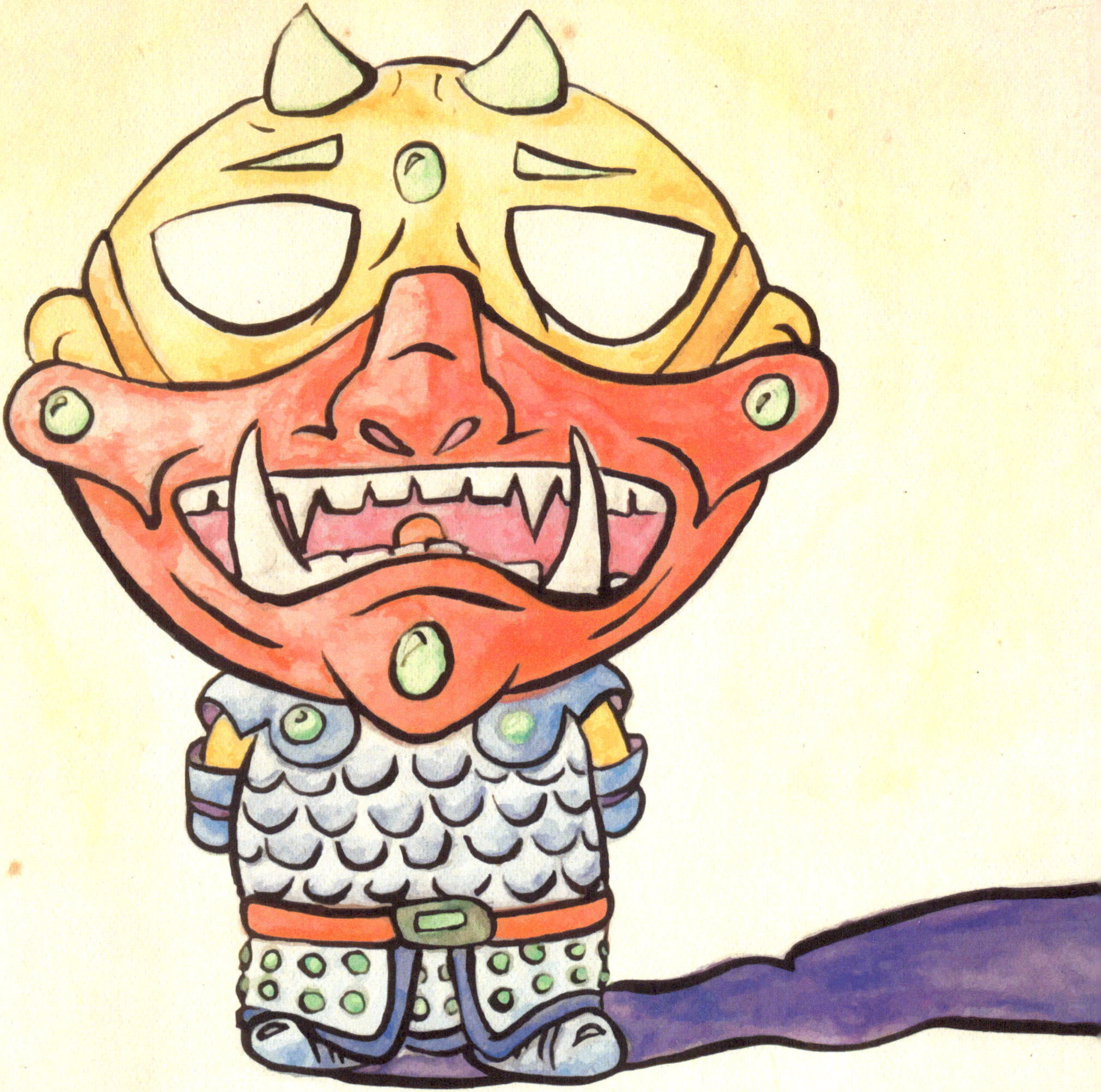

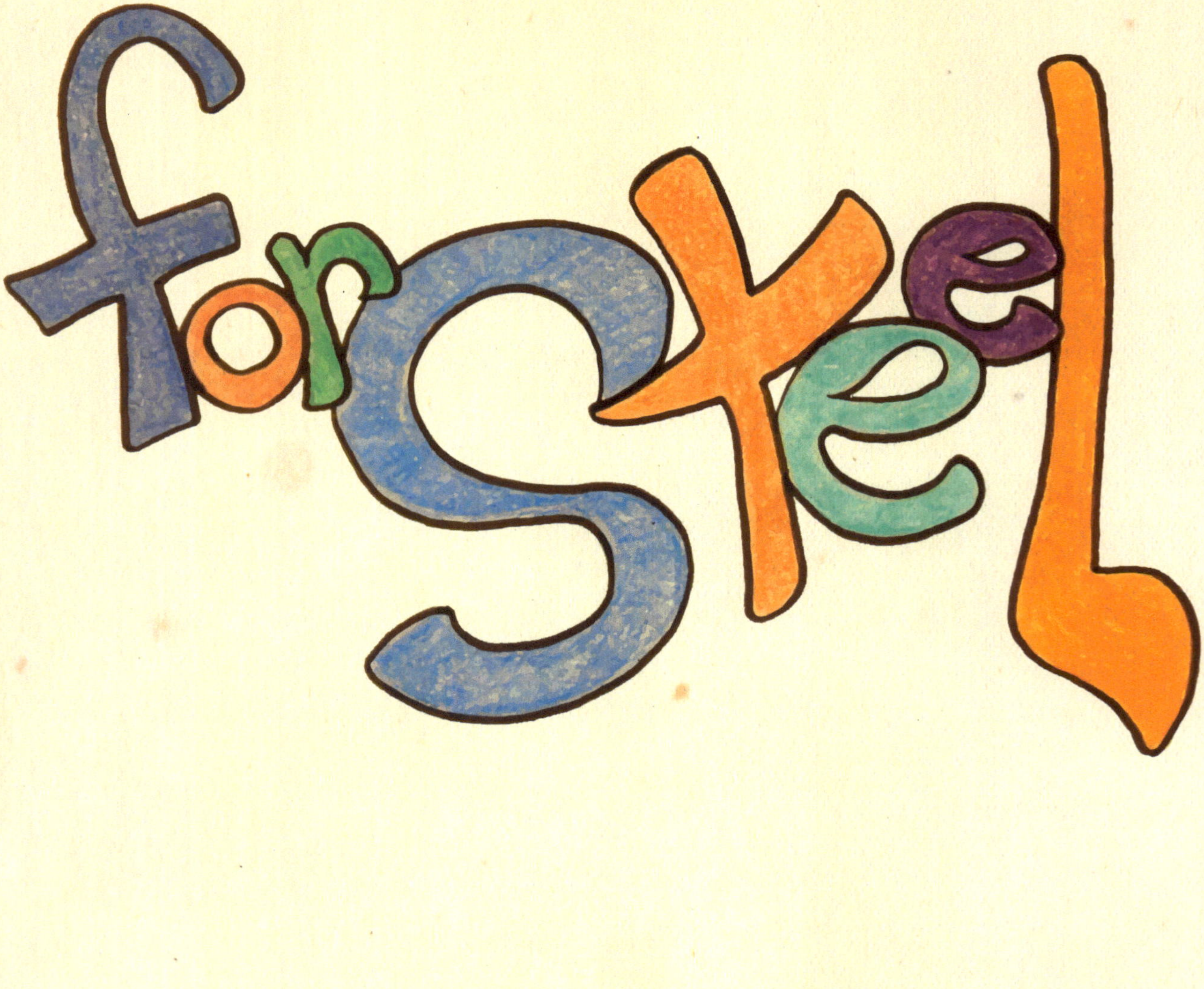
for Steel

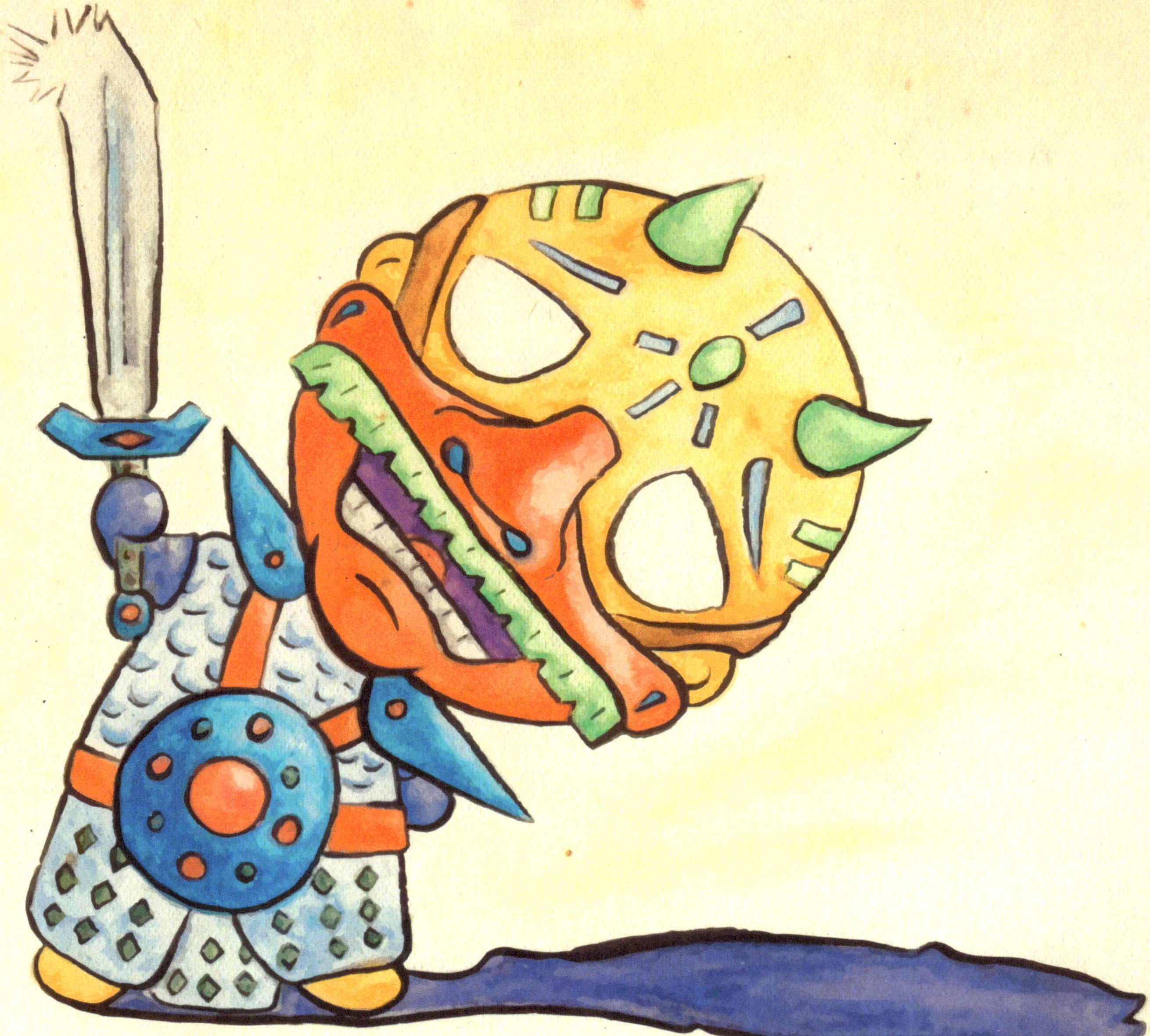

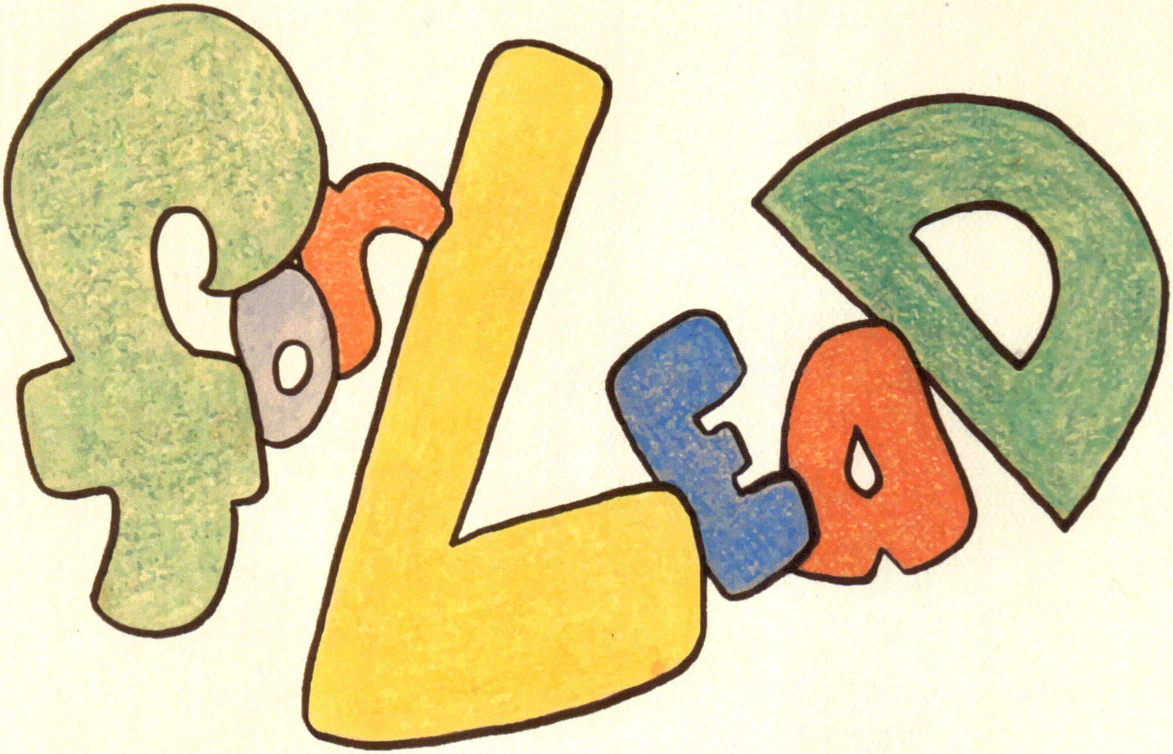
forLeaD

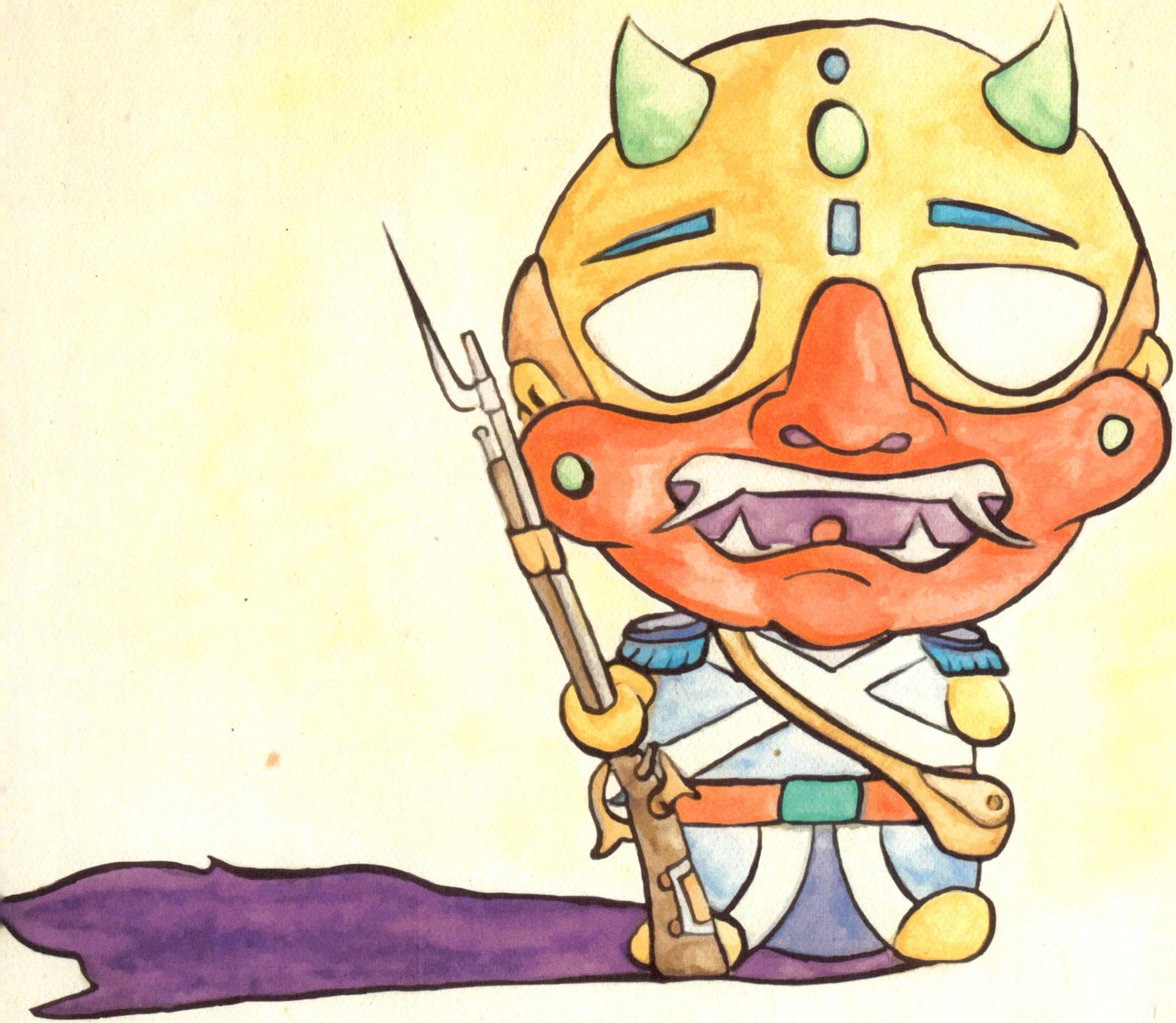

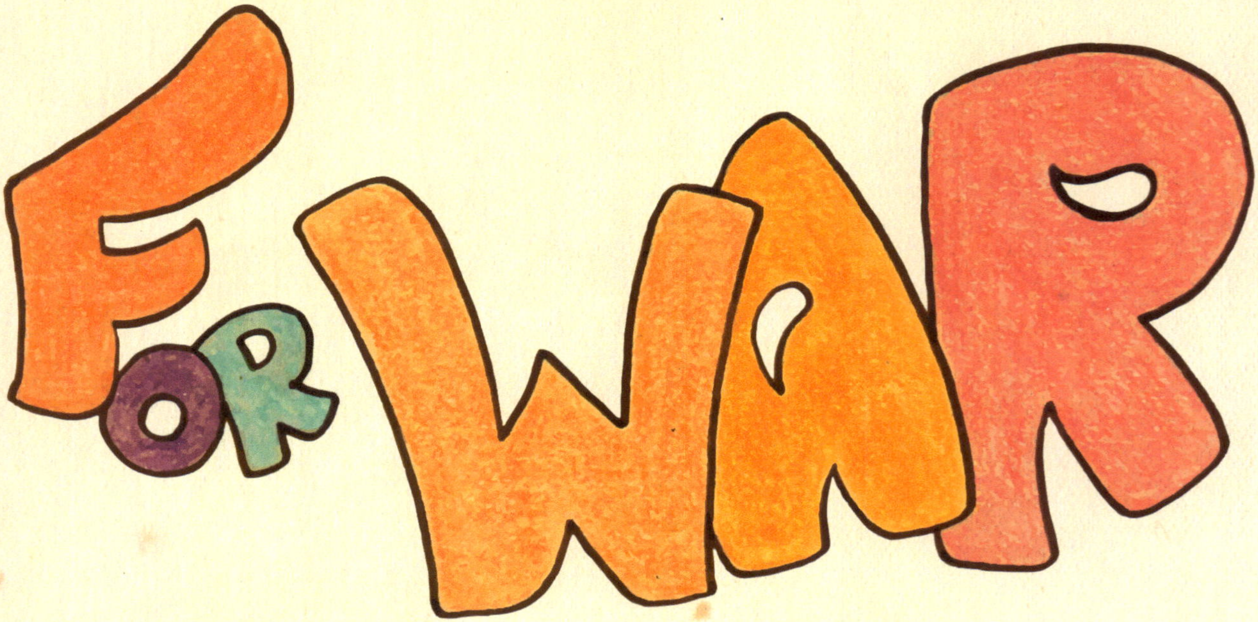
FoR WAR

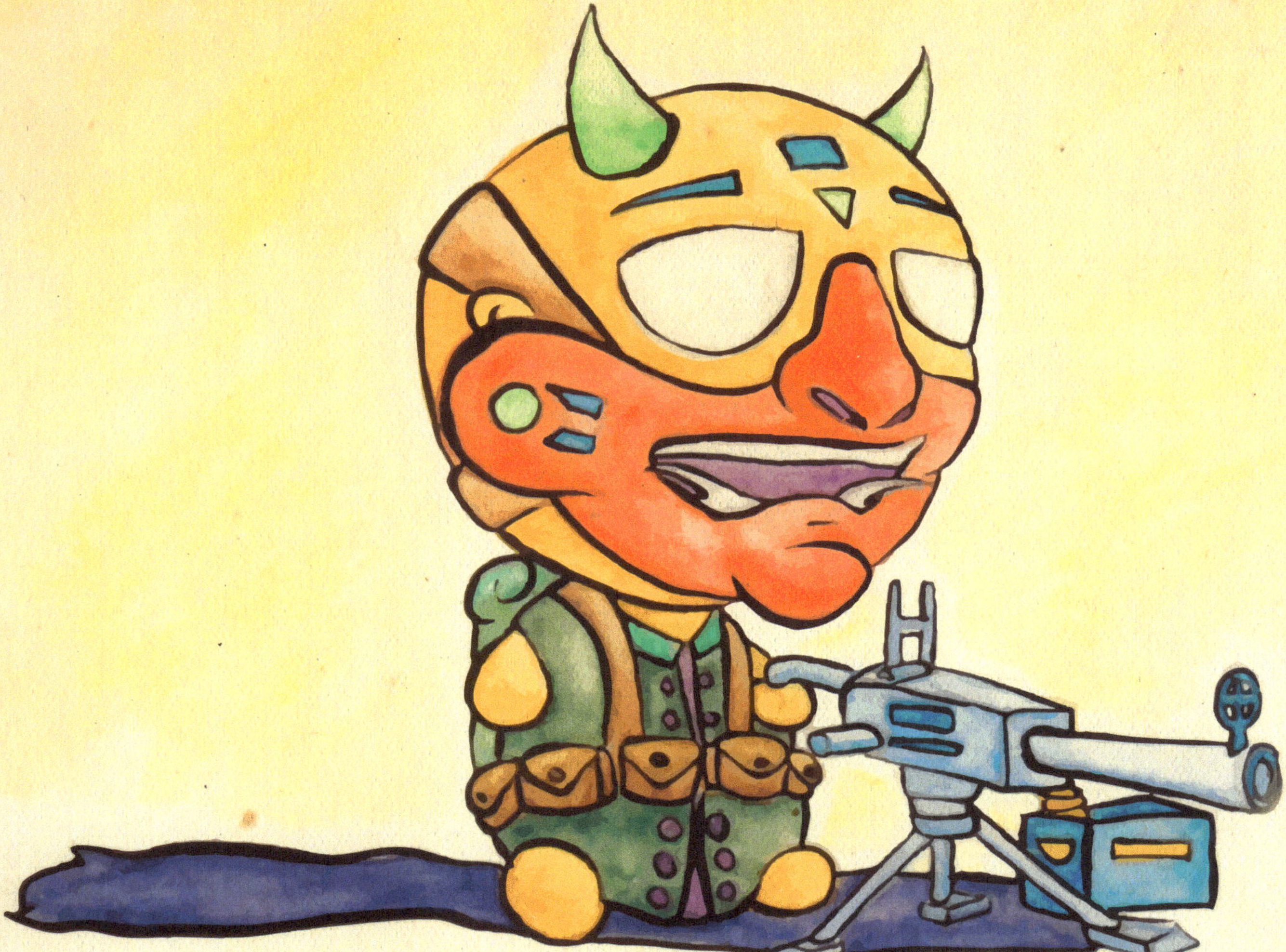

I carry my BANNER

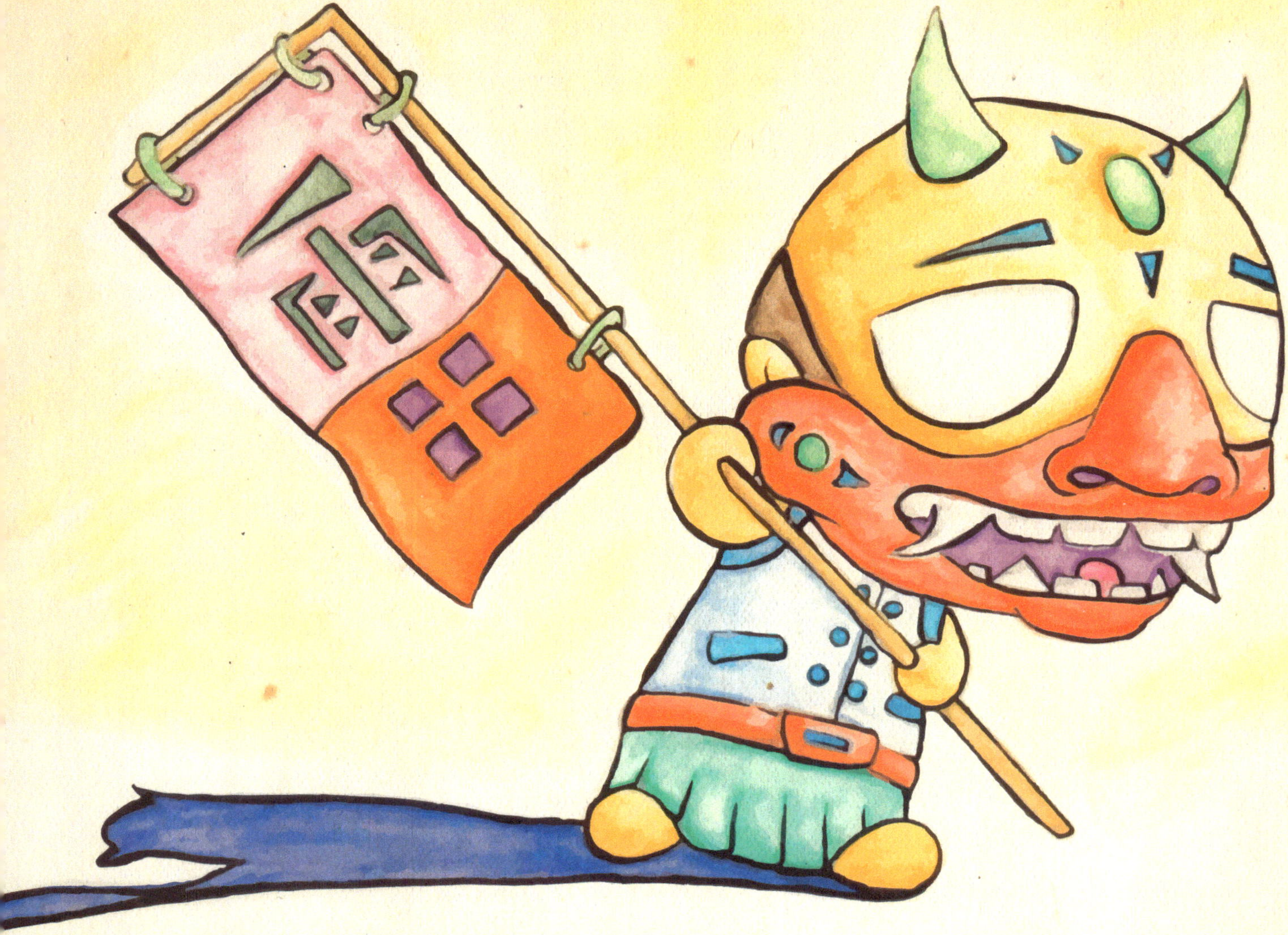
雨

We Lead the Vanguard

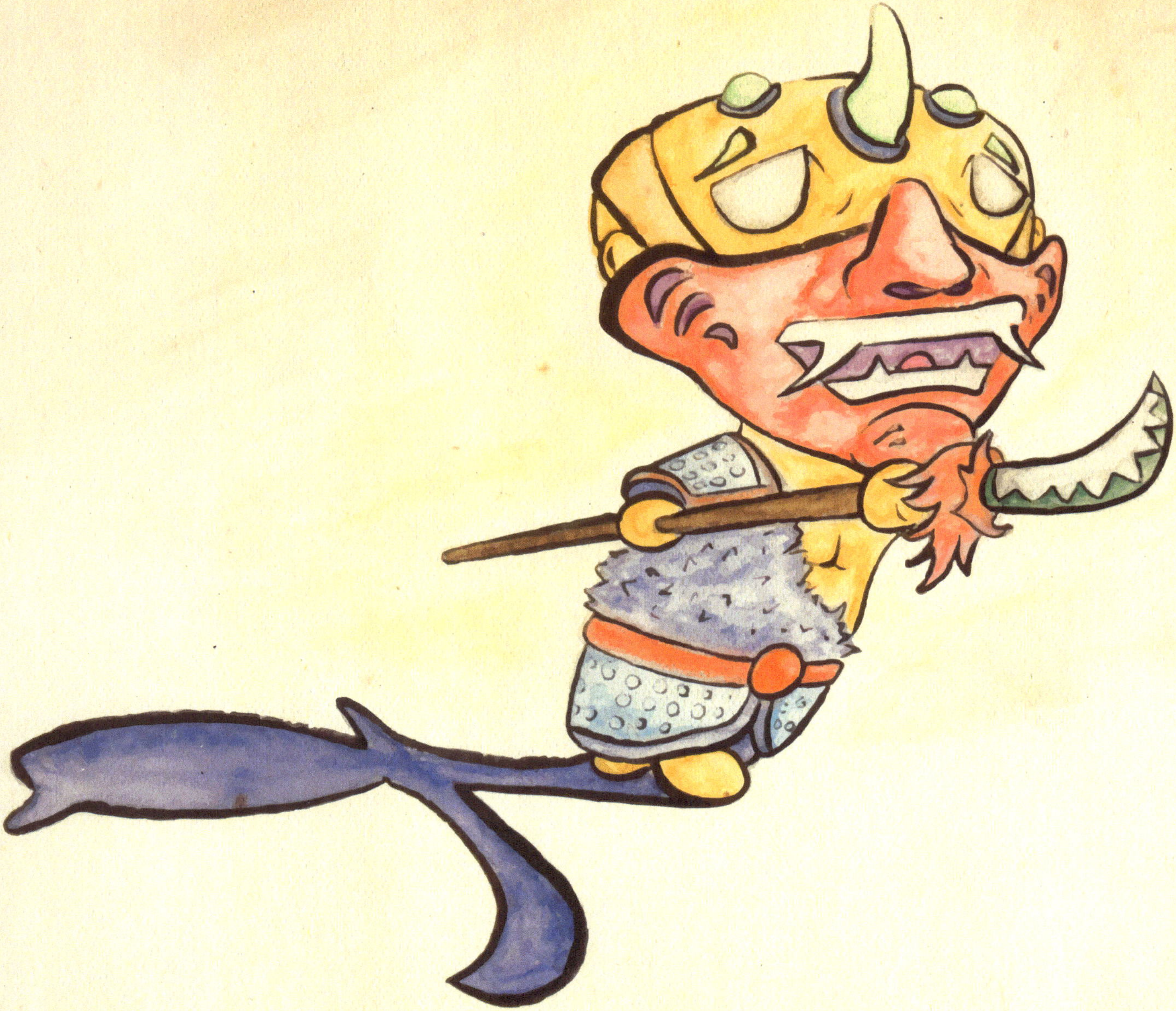

They fear my

BLADE

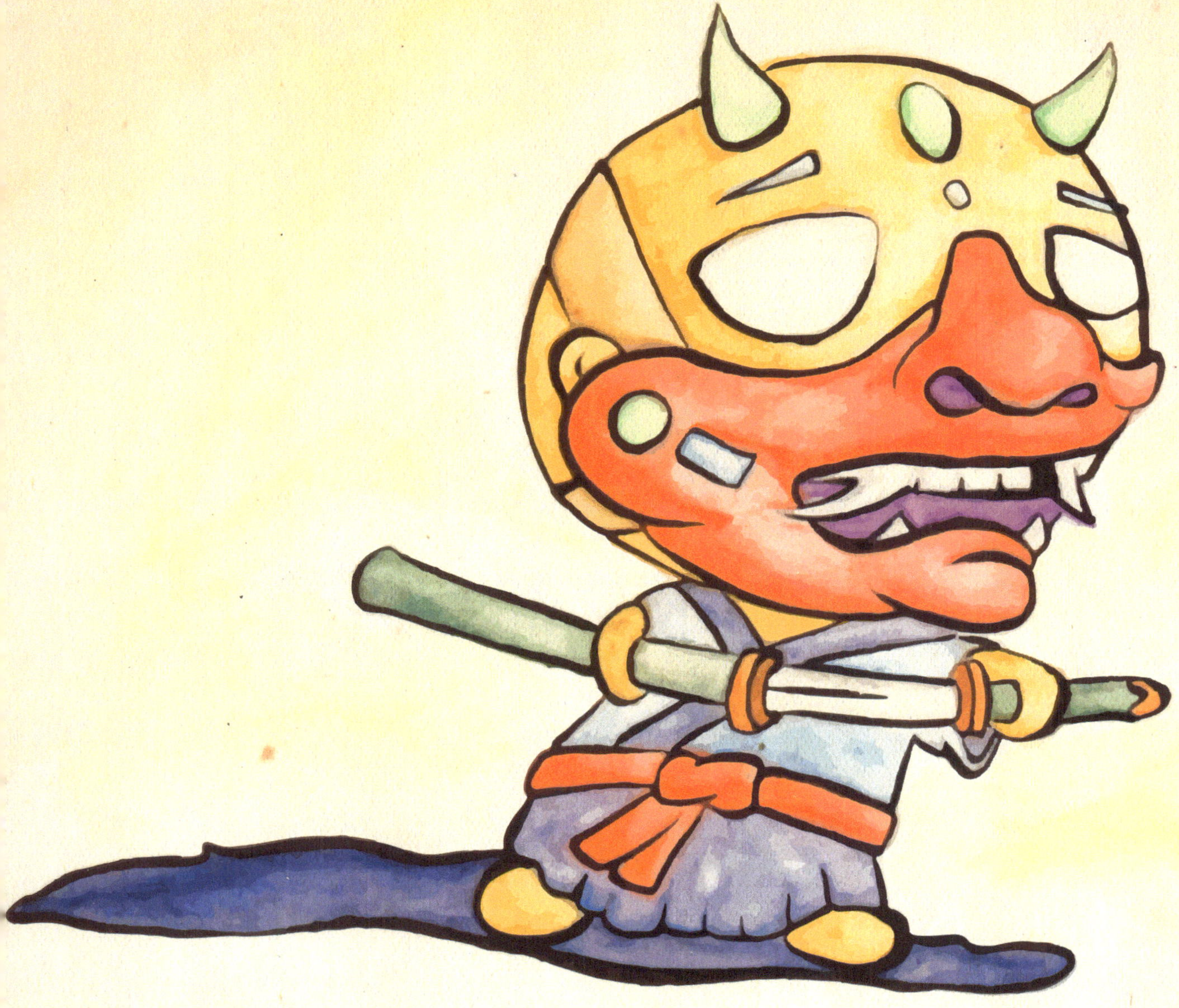

I Scout

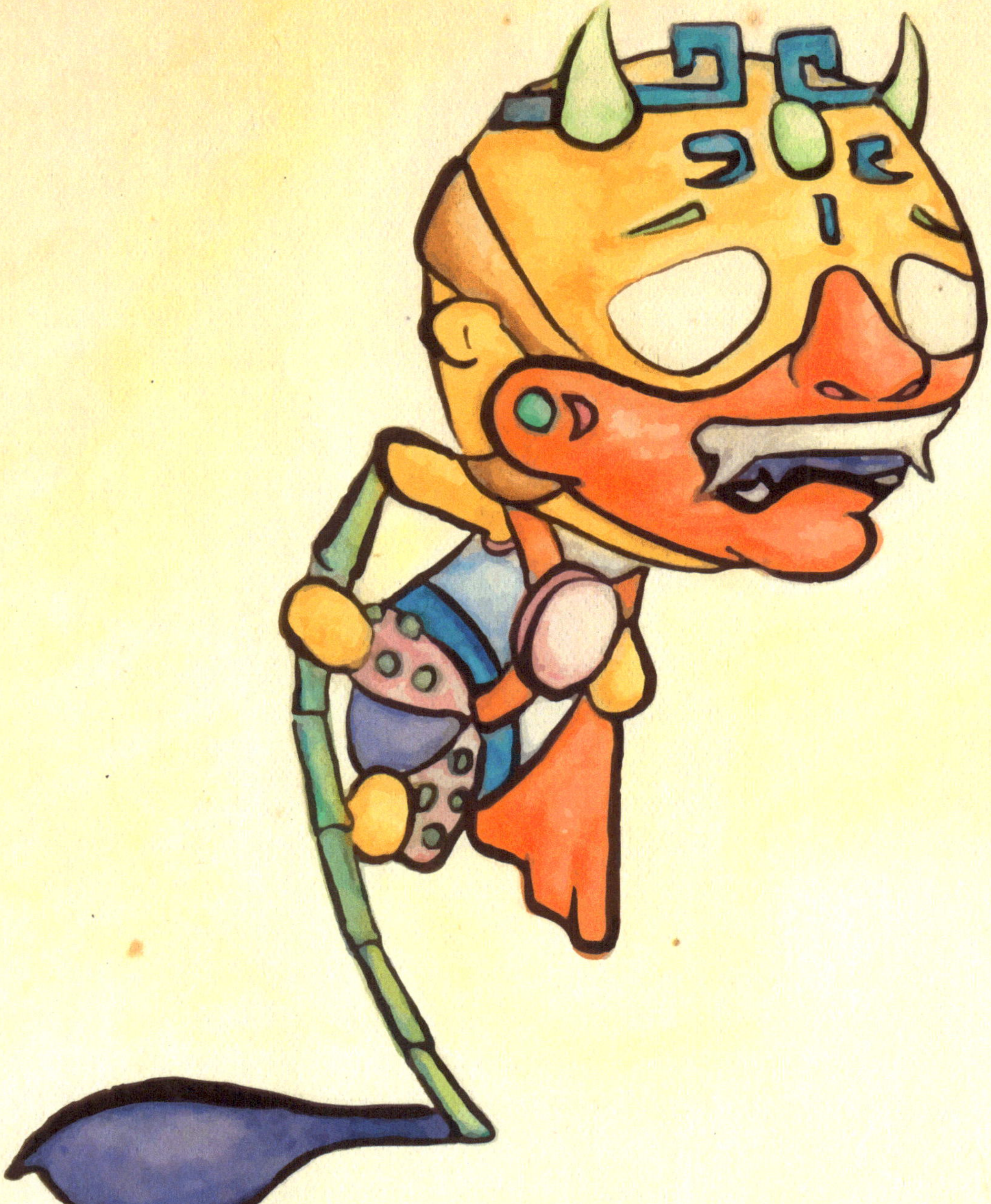

I charge

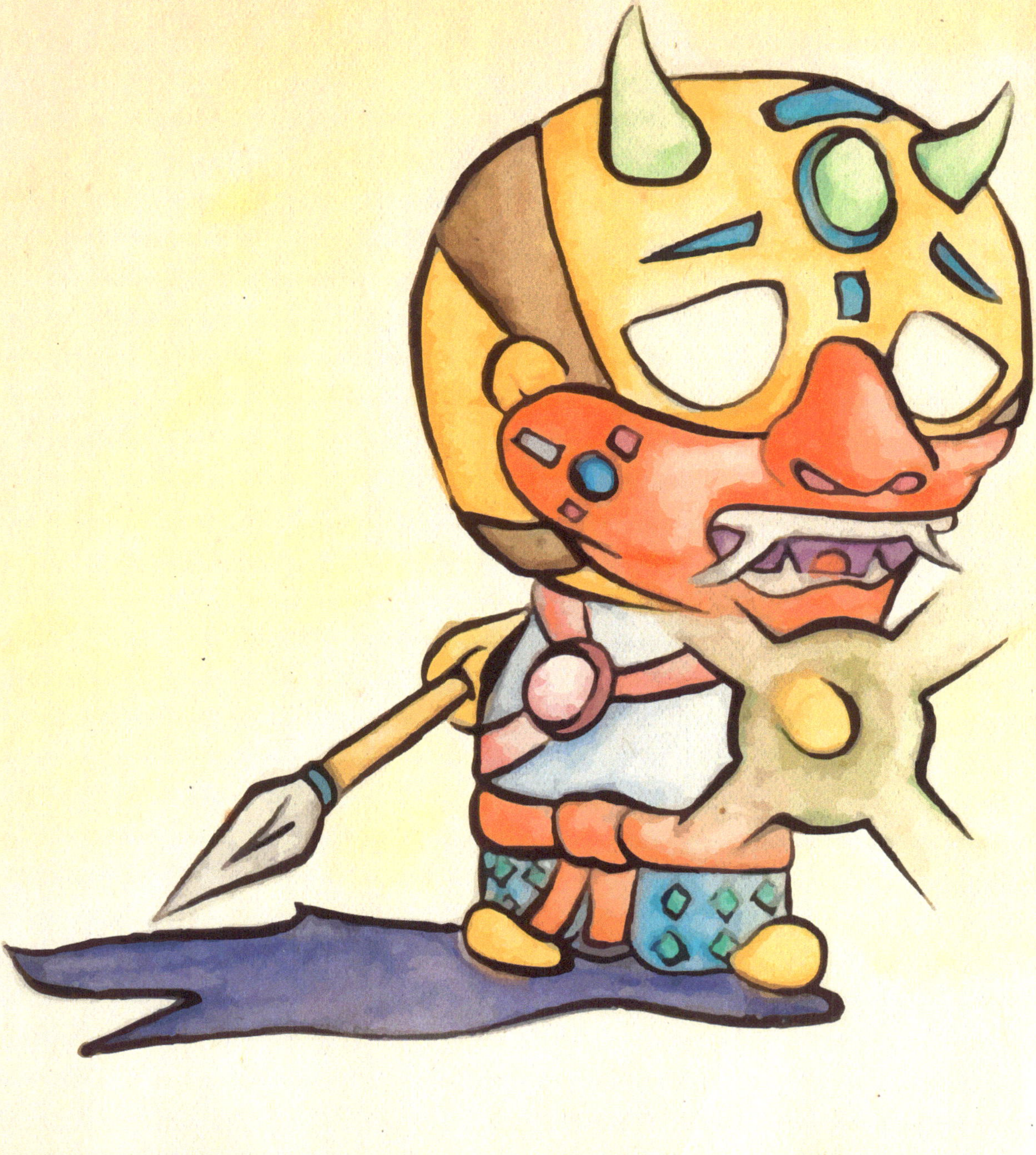

I fly

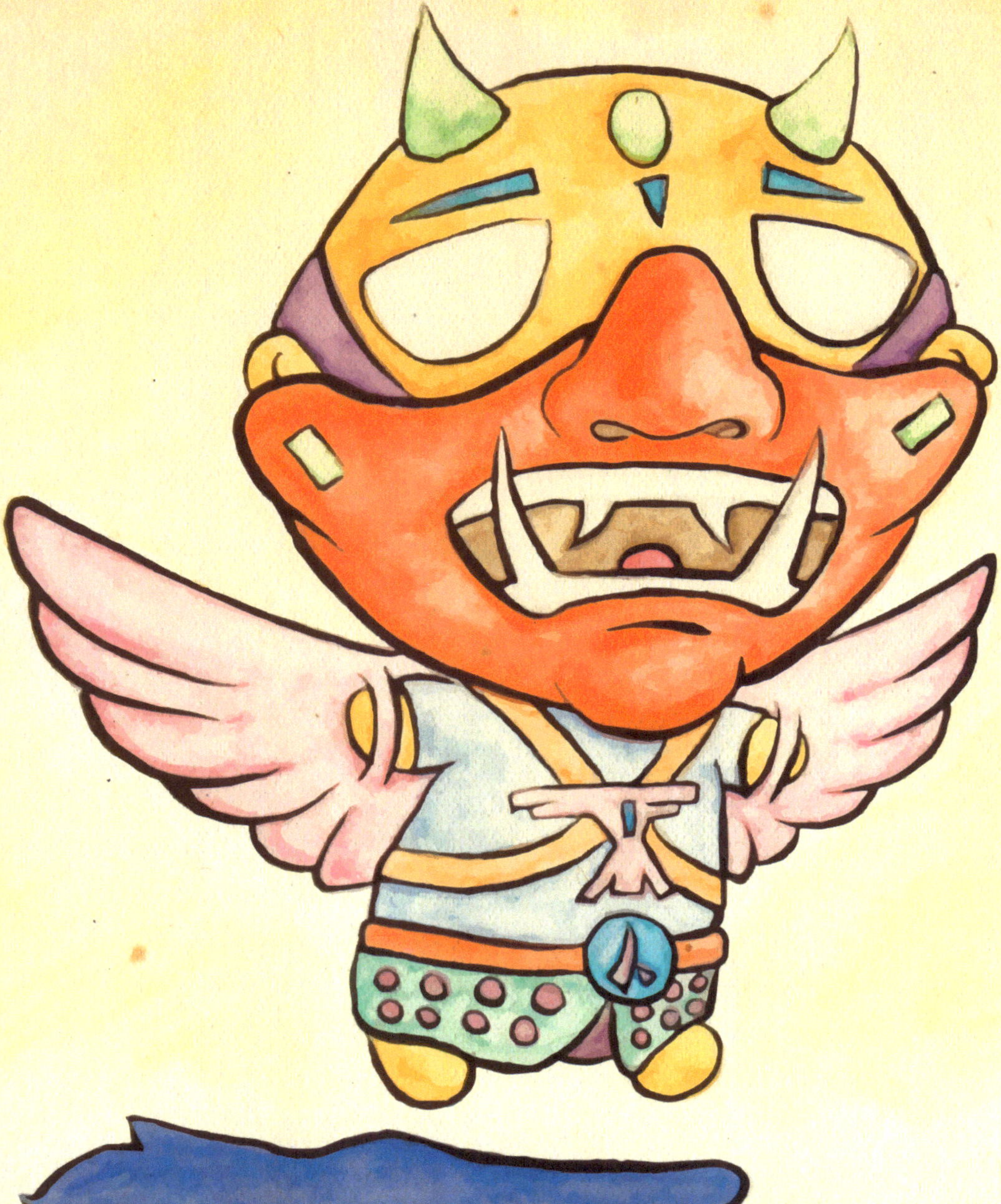

gather your weapons

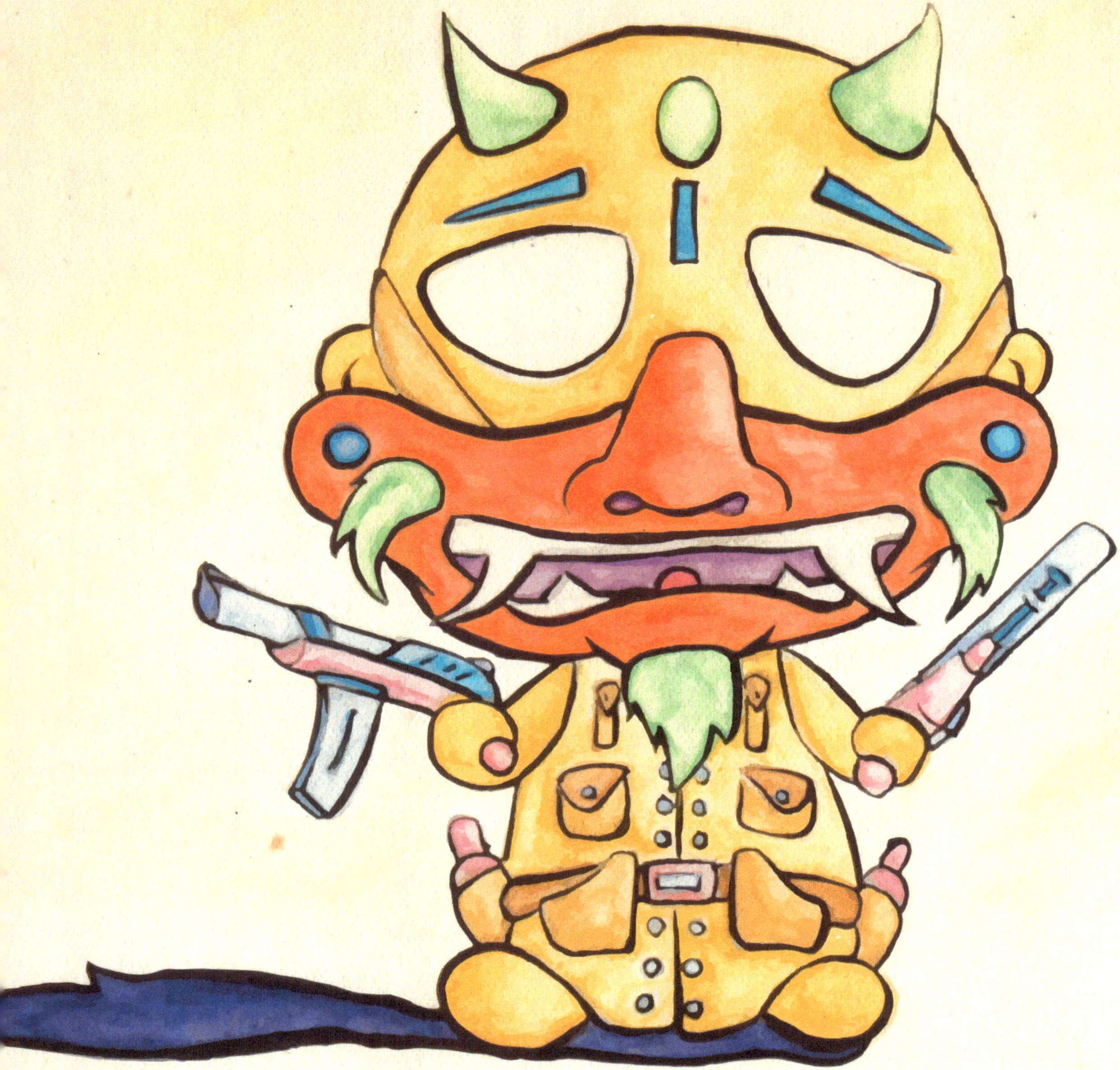

Draw Your FIRE

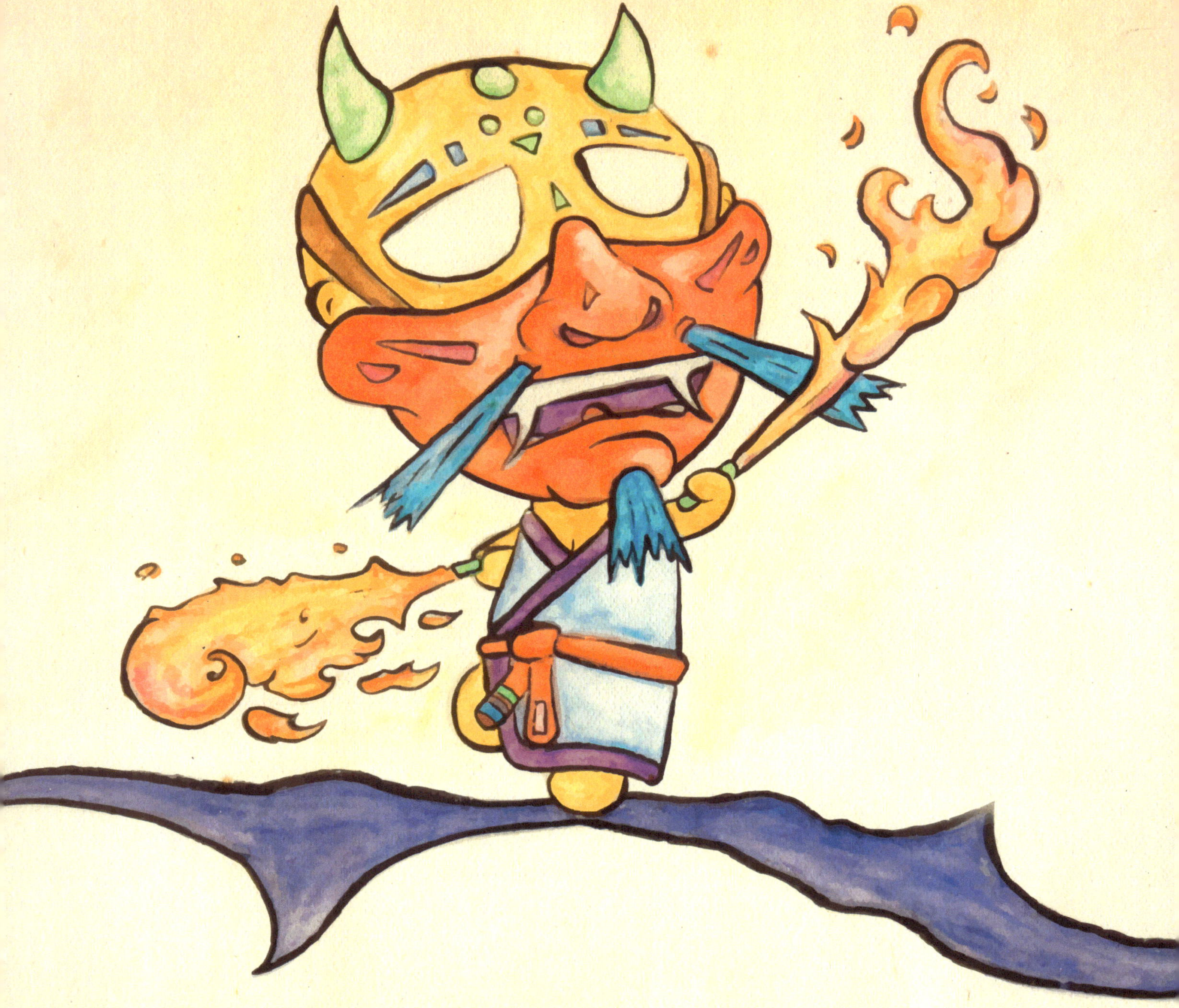

demonstrate
your strength

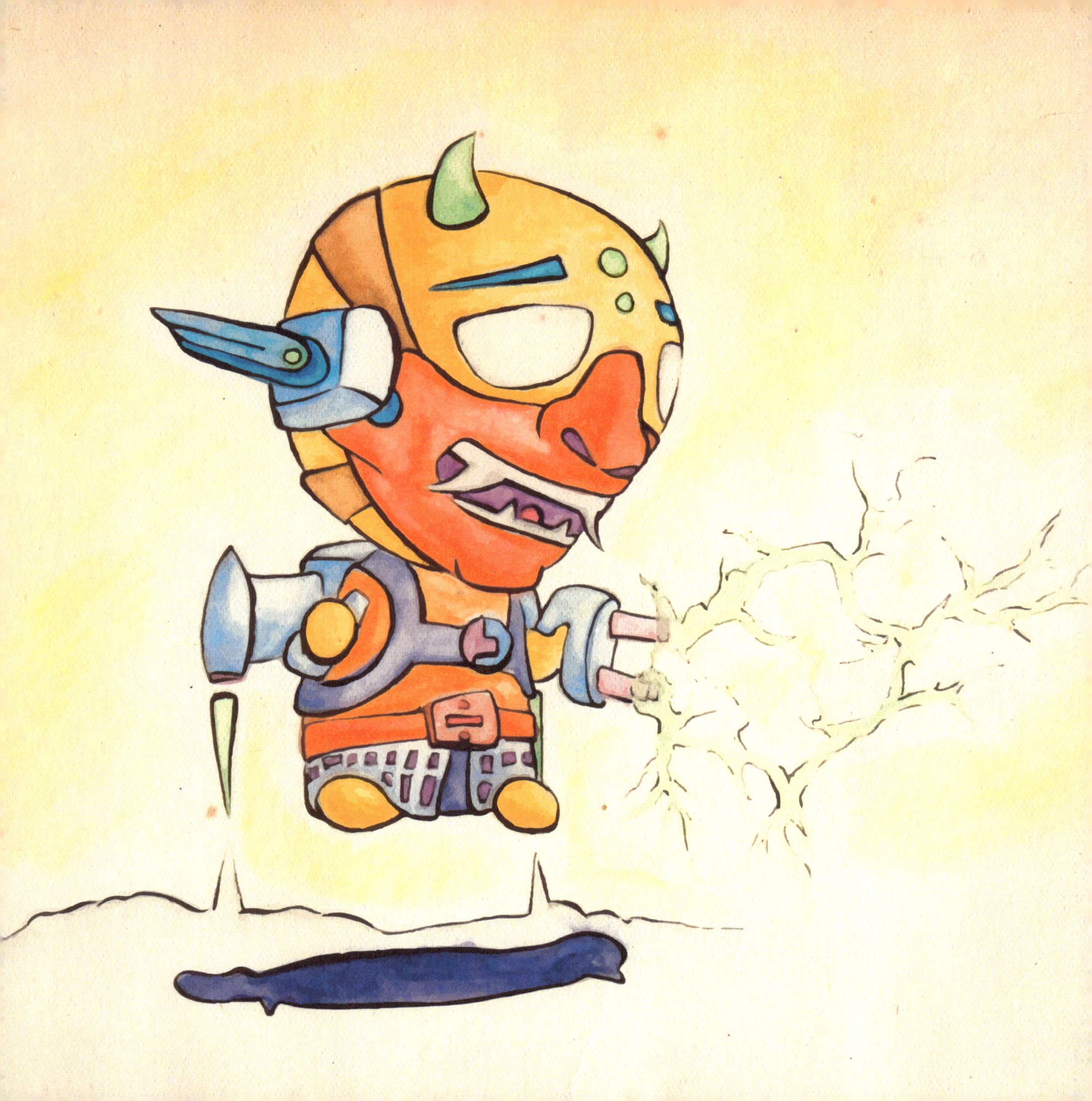

FINDANGER

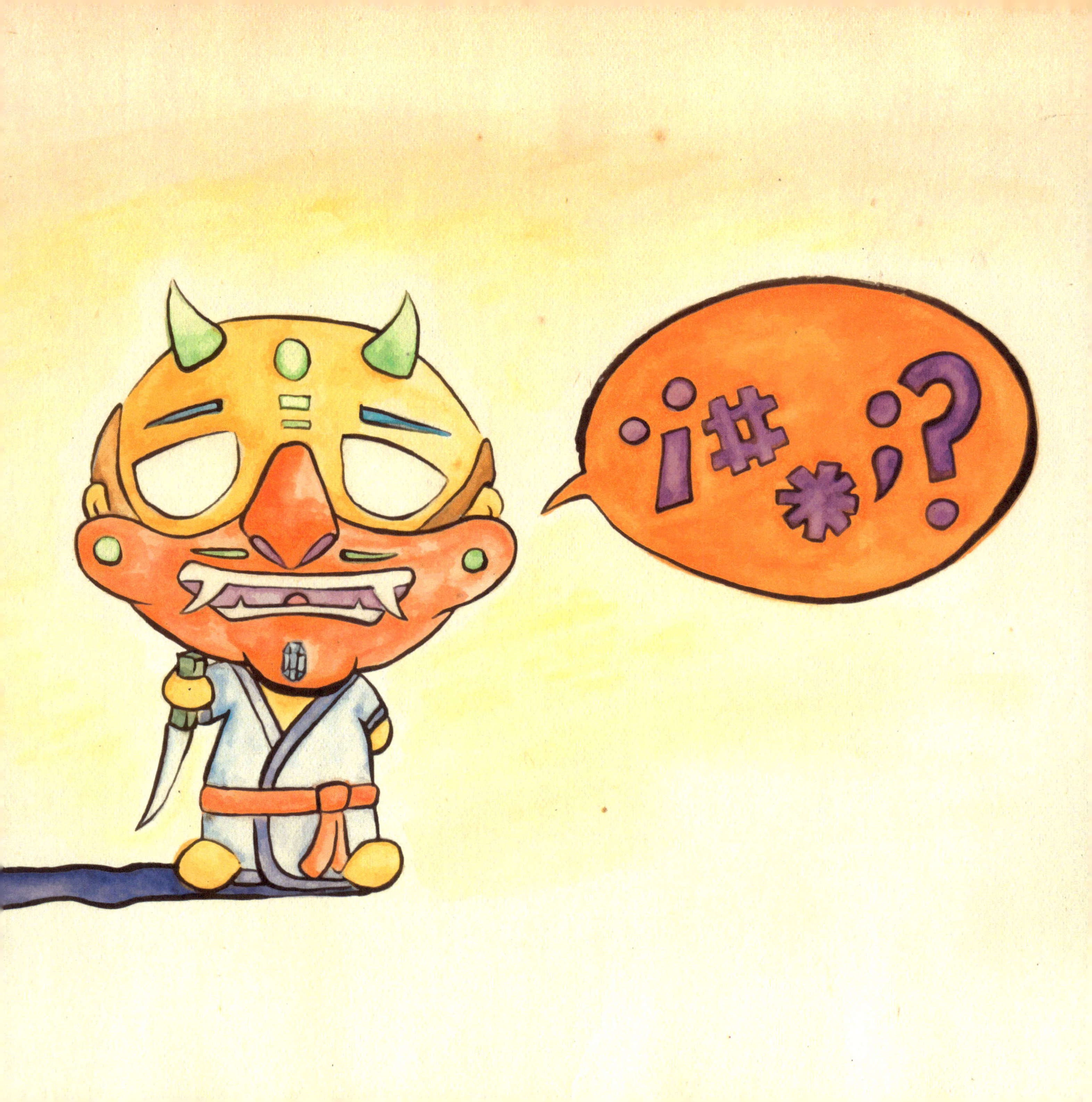

find Peace

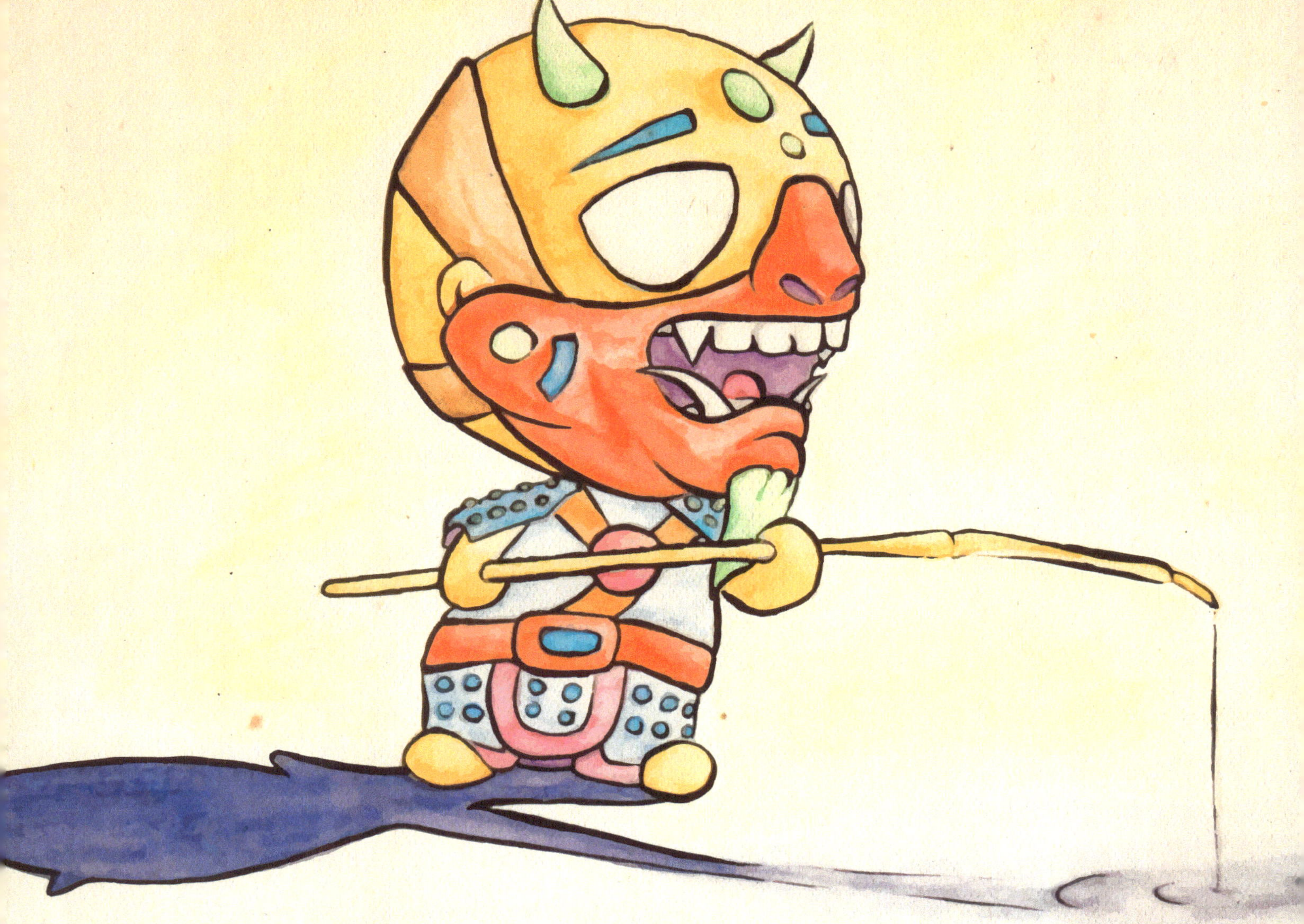

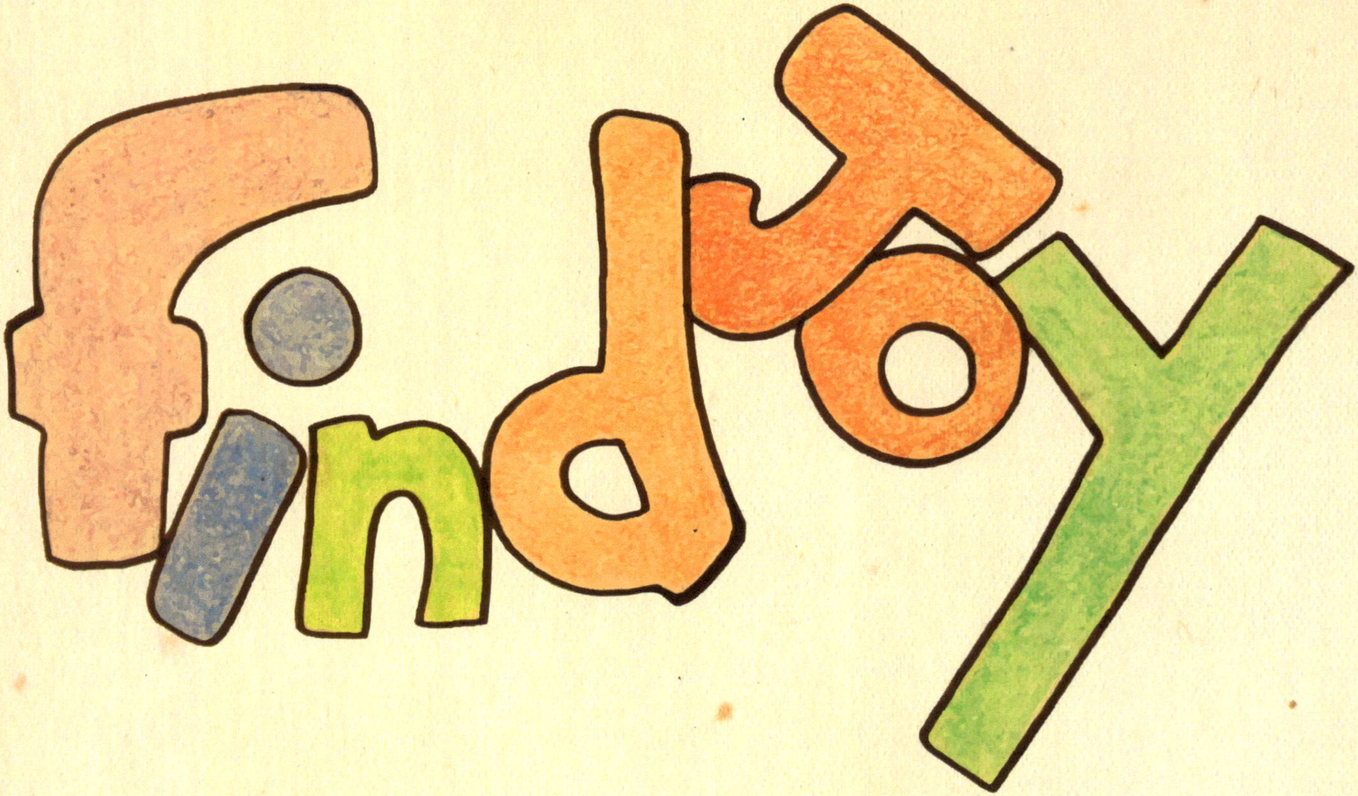
find joy

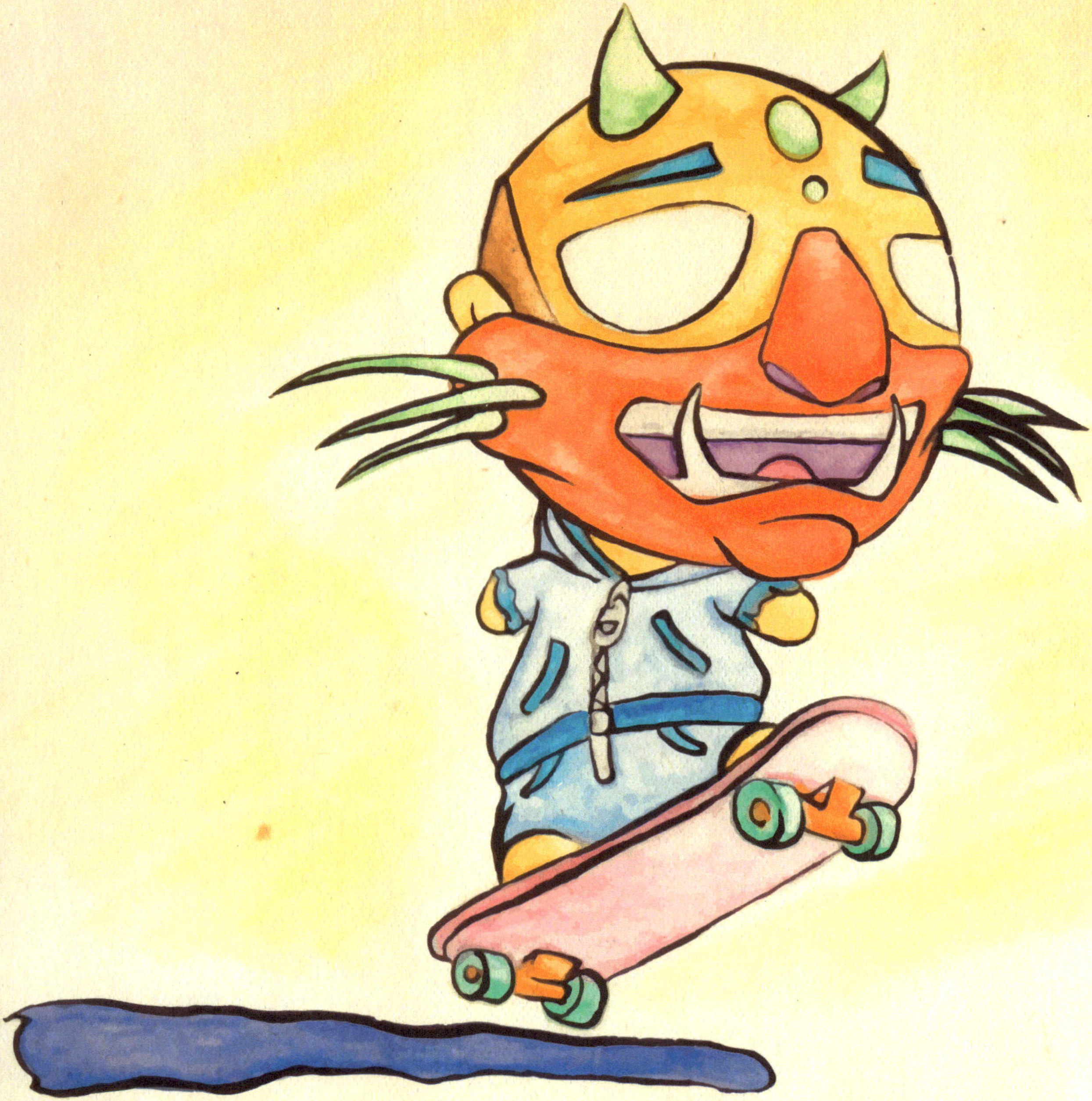

I am Thunder

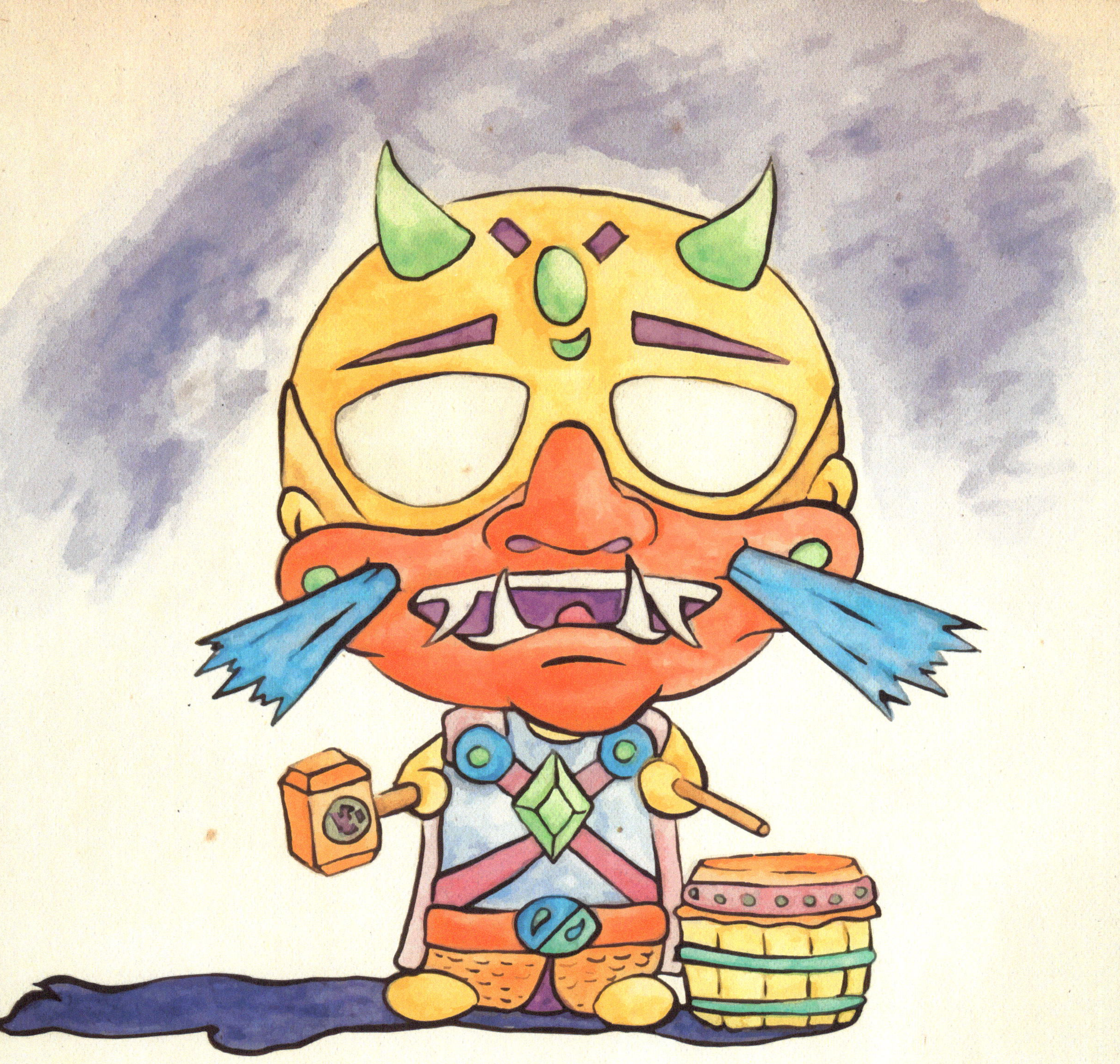

www.ingramcontent.com/pod-product-compliance
Lightning Source LLC
Chambersburg PA
CBHW040753200526
45159CB00025B/2061
9780993838613